CHILDREN 92 PARKER 2004
Egan, Tracie
Cynthia Ann Parker

Ridglea

PRIMARY SOURCES OF
FAMOUS PEOPLE IN AMERICAN HISTORY™

CYNTHIA ANN PARKER

COMANCHE CAPTIVE

TRACIE EGAN

rosen central
Primary Source™
The Rosen Publishing Group, Inc., New York

Published in 2004 by The Rosen Publishing Group, Inc.
29 East 21st Street, New York, NY 10010

Library of Congress Cataloging-in-Publication Data

Egan, Tracie.
Cynthia Ann Parker / Tracie Egan. — 1st ed.
    p. cm. — (Primary sources of famous people in American history)
Summary: A biography of the pioneer woman who as a child was captured and raised by the Comanche Indians.
Includes bibliographical references and index.
ISBN 0-8239-4107-8 (lib. bdg.)
ISBN 0-8239-4179-5 (pbk. bdg.)
6-pack ISBN 0-8239-4306-2
1. Parker, Cynthia Ann, 1827?–1864—Juvenile literature. 2. Indian captivities—Texas—Juvenile literature. 3. Comanche Indians—Juvenile literature. 4. Texas—Biography—Juvenile literature. [1. Parker, Cynthia Ann, 1827?–1864. 2. Comanche Indians—Biography. 3. Indians of North America—Texas—Biography. 4. Indian captivities—Texas. 5. Women—Biography.]
I. Title. II. Series: Primary sources of famous people in American history (New York, N.Y.)
E99.C85 P373 2003
976.4004'9745—dc21

2002152841

Manufactured in the United States of America

Photo credits: cover, p. 8 Lawrence T. Jones III collection, Austin, TX; p. 4 courtesy of Arizona Historical Society, Tucson; p. 5 © Huntington Library/SuperStock, Inc.; p. 7 Library of Congress Prints and Photographs Division; pp. 9, 29 Texas State Library and Archives Commission; pp. 11, 16 © Corbis; p. 12 © Hulton/Archive/Getty Images; pp. 13, 17, 19 Smithsonian American Art Museum, Washington, DC/Art Resource, NY; pp. 14 (X-32201), 24 (X-32185), 25 (X-32238), 28 (X-32234) Denver Public Library, Western History Collection; pp. 15, 21, 23 (bottom) Western History Collection, University of Oklahoma; p. 23 (top) courtesy George Barnard Papers, the Texas Collection, Baylor University, Waco, TX; p. 27 courtesy of Joseph E. Taulman Collection, Center for American History, The University of Texas at Austin, CN 04515.

Designer: Thomas Forget; Photo Researcher: Rebecca Anguin-Cohen

CONTENTS

1 FORT PARKER

Cynthia Ann Parker, a pioneer of the American West, was a white captive of the Comanche, a Native American tribe. Cynthia Ann learned to love life with her tribe and was devoted to her Native American husband and children. Her son Quanah helped to establish peace between white people and Native Americans.

A group of Native American women with a white baby girl. Abduction of children was not uncommon in time of war.

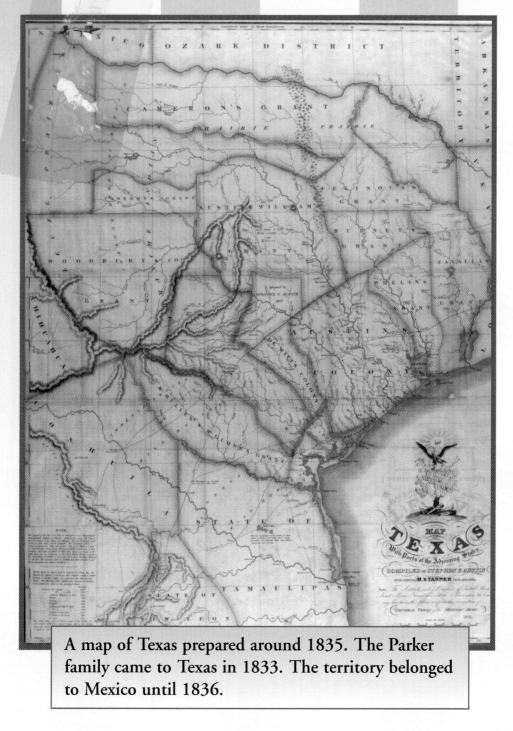

A map of Texas prepared around 1835. The Parker family came to Texas in 1833. The territory belonged to Mexico until 1836.

Cynthia Ann Parker was born in the 1820s in Illinois. In 1833, the Parkers and some other families traveled in covered wagons from Illinois to Texas. They were looking to make new homes in the unsettled land. In Texas, the families built a fort. It was called Fort Parker.

THE REPUBLIC OF TEXAS

The Mexican government invited Americans to settle in its northern territories. But by 1836, those Americans were unhappy with the Mexican government and rebelled. Texas was the only territory to be an independent republic before it became a state.

This colored engraving shows a family of settlers moving west in a covered wagon. The Parker family, like many others, came west to own land and to farm.

The families feared that Native Americans would raid Fort Parker. They built high walls and gates to protect themselves from the Native Americans. The gates were always kept locked. But by May 1836, no one had seen any Native Americans in months. Keeping the gates locked no longer seemed important.

A photograph of Elisha Anglin, who was at Fort Parker on the day of the raid when Cynthia Ann was kidnapped. He and his brother removed the arrows from the body of Cynthia Ann's father.

A modern re-creation of Fort Parker, near Groesbeck, Texas. Cynthia Ann Parker was kidnapped by the Comanche from this fort on May 19, 1836.

One day the men were out working the fields. The gates were left open. Suddenly, Fort Parker was invaded by Native Americans. The Native Americans killed several people, including Cynthia Ann's cousin, her uncle, and her father. They took five captives, including Cynthia Ann, who was about nine, and her brother, John, who was six.

A NATIVE AMERICAN NAME

The Comanche gave Cynthia Ann Parker a new name, Naduah. It is a Comanche word for "keeps warm with us." It is the name she used for most of her life.

This sensationalized engraving reveals the common fear among western settlers that Native Americans would break into their homes and kidnap them.

Some captives were tortured and beaten. A few of them were sold to other tribes as slaves. John Parker was sent to live with a band of Kiowa. Cynthia was taken to live with a band of Comanche.

This sensationalized magazine illustration shows Native Americans, having attacked a wagon train of settlers, gambling over possession of a female captive.

Comanche War Party, painted by George Catlin, 1837. Like other Plains tribes, the Comanche had adopted the horse from the Spanish and built their whole culture around it.

2 LIFE AS A COMANCHE

In the beginning, things were very hard for Cynthia Ann. She missed her family. But the Comanche were kind to her. She was given to a Comanche couple. They treated Cynthia as if she were their daughter. They dressed her in Native American clothing and fed her well.

A studio portrait of two Comanche women showing their style of dress

Comanche women and a child in front of a tepee. Photography was being perfected in the years after the Civil War, so some photographs of Native American life have survived.

Cynthia played with the other Native American children and began to learn their ways. She learned how to soak bark to tan leather. She also learned how to cook and how to embroider clothes with beads. The memory of her old life began to fade.

Native American children playing a game, 1872. Cynthia Ann played such games and learned the ways of her Comanche captors.

A Comanche Village, painted by George Catlin, 1835. The women in the foreground are drying meat and preparing hides.

Peta Nacona, a Comanche war chief, wanted to marry Cynthia. He brought a group of horses to Cynthia's adoptive parents as a gift. When she was 18, Cynthia Ann married Peta Nacona. Cynthia went on raids and hunting trips with her new husband.

A NATIVE AMERICAN MARRIAGE

Most Native American men took more than one wife. Cynthia Ann Parker's husband, Peta Nacona, wished to be married only to Cynthia. It was a sign of great devotion.

Comanche Indians Chasing Buffalo with Lances and Bows, painted by George Catlin, 1848. The buffalo provided the Comanche with food and shelter.

In 1845, Cynthia gave birth to their first child, a boy. They named him Quanah. They had a second son, Pecos. Later they had a daughter, Topsannah. Women living on the frontier did not have many children because of the rough conditions. Cynthia was honored and prized among Native American women because she had three children.

DID YOU KNOW?

The name of Cynthia's first child, Quanah, means "fragrance." Her daughter's name, Topsannah, means "prairie flower."

A photograph of Quanah Parker, Cynthia Ann's surviving son, sitting beside a portrait of his mother and sister.

3 SEPARATED FROM FAMILY AGAIN

On December 18, 1860, Cynthia and Nacona were on a hunting trip with their band of Comanche. Texas Ranger Lawrence Sullivan Ross and his soldiers invaded their camp. Nacona, Quanah, and Pecos managed to escape. Cynthia and her daughter, Topsannah, were captured.

A HOLLYWOOD STORY

The story of the abduction of Cynthia Ann Parker was the basis for the western movie *The Searchers*, starring John Wayne and directed by John Ford.

Top left, a photograph of Lawrence Sullivan
Ross, the Texas Ranger who attacked the
Comanche hunting camp at Mule Creek and
discovered Cynthia Ann Parker. Below, a
company of Texas Rangers.

Cynthia's skin had darkened from the sun. Her once blonde hair was now dirty and greasy. She looked like she was a Native American. However, Captain Ross looked in her eyes and saw that they were blue. He remembered the story of the missing girl. He wrote to Cynthia's surviving family.

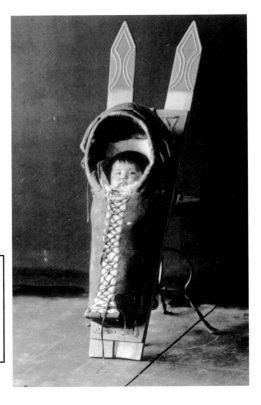

Comanche cradle boards were used to carry very young children.

A photograph of Cynthia Ann Parker holding her daughter, Topsannah, which means "prairie flower"

Colonel Isaac Parker, an uncle, arrived to claim Cynthia, but she remembered very little English. But Cynthia recognized her name when she heard it. "Me Cynthia," she said. Cynthia and Topsannah were then taken back to Texas to be with the Parkers.

HIS WORD WAS HIS PLEDGE

Cynthia taught her children about honor and the importance of promises. When Quanah Parker was making peace with the white people, he never signed a treaty. He would not make a promise that he couldn't keep.

Taulman · HUBBARD CITY, TEXAS.

Isaac Parker, a surviving relative to whom Cynthia Ann was returned when she was taken from her Native American family

Cynthia tried to escape many times. Each time she was caught and returned to the Parkers. In 1863, her son Pecos and her daughter, Topsannah, died. Cynthia was struck with grief and starved herself to death in 1870.

Of her Comanche family, only Quanah survived. He became a legendary warrior chief.

Quanah Parker's family. Quanah Parker became a successful businessman and negotiated a treaty between his people and the U.S. government.

DEPARTMENT OF THE INTERIOR,

UNITED STATES INDIAN SERVICE,

Cache, Okla.

July 22rd, 1909.

Governor Campbell.
  Austin, Texas.

Dear sir,

Congress has set aside money for me to remove the body of my mother Cynthia Ann Parker and build a monument and some time pasted I was hunting in Texas and they accused me killing antelope and I am afraid to come for fear they might make some trouble for me because of a dislike to a friend of mine in Texas, would you protect me if I was to come to Austin and neighborhood to remove my mother's body some time soon.

Yours very truly

Quanah Parker

A letter from Quanah Parker to the government asking for protection in moving the body from his mother's grave

TIMELINE

1820s—Cynthia Ann Parker is born in Illinois.

1833—The Parker family moves west to settle in Texas.

1836—Cynthia Ann is kidnapped by a Comanche raiding party.

1840—Cynthia Ann marries Peta Nacona, a Comanche war chief.

1845—Cynthia Ann gives birth to Quanah, her first child.

1860—Texas Ranger Lawrence Sullivan Ross recaptures Cynthia Ann from the Comanche.

1863—Cynthia Ann's younger son, Pecos, and daughter, Topsannah, die.

1870—Cynthia Ann dies.

GLOSSARY

accustomed (uh-CUS-tumd) Being used to something.

captive (KAP-tihv) A person who is taken prisoner.

colonel (KER-nul) A military officer.

Comanche (kuh-MAN-chee) A Native American tribe.

frontier (fruhn-TIHR) The far edge of a country where few people live.

pioneers (pye-un-NEERZ) People who explore unknown territories and settle there.

raid (RAYD) A surprise attack, in which the attacker steals goods or harms property.

relative (REH-luh-tiv) A family member connected by blood or marriage.

WEB SITES

Due to the changing nature of Internet links, the Rosen Publishing Group, Inc., has developed an online list of Web sites related to the subject of this book. This site is updated regularly. Please use this link to access the list:

http://www.rosenlinks.com/fpah/capa

PRIMARY SOURCE IMAGE LIST

Page 5: A map of Texas prepared in 1835 by Stephen F. Austin.
Page 7: *Immigrants Crossing the Plains*, an engraving by F. Darley, now with the Library of Congress.
Page 8: Photograph of Elisha Anglin.
Page 9: A photograph of restored Fort Parker, from the Texas State Library.
Page 11: *Widow Scraggs Defends Her Home*, engraved in 1883.
Page 12: *Raid on the Oregon Trail*, from *Harper's Weekly*, 1870.
Page 13: *Comanche War Party*, by George Catlin, 1837, oil on canvas, now with the Smithsonian Institution.
Page 16: Indian children playing, photographed by John K. Hillers, 1872, in northern Arizona.
Page 17: *A Comanche Village*, by George Catlin, 1835, now with the Smithsonian Institution.
Page 19: *Comanche Indians Chasing Buffalo with Lances and Bows*, by George Catlin, 1848, oil on canvas, now with the Smithsonian Institution.
Page 21: Quanah Parker.
Page 24: A Comanche cradle board, from the collection of the Denver Public Library.
Page 25: Cynthia Ann Parker, photographed in the 1860s, from *Cynthia Ann Parker: The Story of Her Capture*, by James T. DeShields, 1886.
Page 27: Photograph of Isaac Parker, from the Center for American History, the University of Texas at Austin.

Page 28: Quanah Parker's family, photographed by Alexander Lambert, 1905, from *Scriber's Magazine*, November 1905.
Page 29: Letter written by Quanah Parker, July 22, 1909.

INDEX

ABOUT THE AUTHOR

Tracie Egan is a freelance writer who lives in New York City.